Untended Garden

(Histories and Reinhabitation in Suburbia)

Untended Garden

. ~ ∞

(Histories and Reinhabitation in Suburbia)

Grant Hier

THE POETRY PRESS

Los Angeles Hollywood

THE POETRY PRESS
OF PRESS AMERICANA

http://www.americanpopularculture.com

Library of Congress Cataloging-in-Publication Data

Hier, Grant, 1956-
Untended garden : (histories and reinhabitation in suburbia) / Grant Hier.
pages cm
ISBN 978-0-9829558-9-5
I. Title.
PS3608.I329U58 2015
811'.6--dc23
2014042772

EPIGRAPH

EAST OF EDEN by John Steinbeck (Penguin Classics 2000). Copyright 1952 by John Steinbeck. Copyright © renewed by Elaine Steinbeck, Thom Steinbeck and John Steinbeck IV, 1980. Introduction copyright © Penguin Putnam Inc., 1992.

"Reinhabitation" excerpt by Gary Snyder used with permission from the author.

PHOTOGRAPHS

Cog Stone images: Courtesy of the Bowers Museum, Santa Ana, CA.

Los Angeles, as it appeared in 1850: Courtesy of USC Digital Library.

Santa Ana River Flood, 1916: Courtesy of the Anaheim Heritage Center, Anaheim Public Library.

All cover photography by Grant Hier, courtesy of the author.

For all of the blood, all the way back.

And for Walt.

CONTENTS

Untended Garden

Once, fifty miles down the valley, my father bored a
well. The drill came up first with topsoil and then with
gravel and then with white sea sand full of shells and
even pieces of whalebone. There were twenty feet of
sand and then black earth again, and even a piece of
redwood, that imperishable wood that does not rot.
Before the inland sea the valley must have been a forest.
And those things had happened right under our feet.
And it seemed to me sometimes at night that I could
feel both the sea and the redwood forest before it.

– John Steinbeck, from *East of Eden*

How does knowledge of place help us know the Self?
The answer, simply put, is that we are all composite
beings, not only physically but intellectually, whose sole
individual identifying feature is a particular form or
structure changing constantly in time. There is no "self"
to be found in that, and yet oddly enough, there is… no
self-realization without the Whole Self, and the whole
self is the whole thing. Thus, knowing who and where
are intimately linked.

– Gary Snyder, from "Reinhabitation"

i.

(Unnoticed Settling:
Unknown Season)

.

This neighborhood
is filled with birds:

the plaintive call
of a mourning dove

and the distant response
from a wire unseen,

two crows on grass
that bob and caw as one –

and the single mockingbird
chants a single word.

The sky is stitched
with a tapestry of coos and chirps,

tweeps and caws,
threads of song

that lace
the leaves.

I step from under the shelter
of the central Modesto Ash tree,
out into the sprinkling mist.

A brown thrush perched on brick under the eaves
watches, twisted root fragment corkscrewing
from her beak, remnant of an orange tree

now forty years dead, but the song
of the warbler's ancestor
still vibrates in the zigzag hum of grain.

I nod at her, pace the perimeter of the yard,

one footfall for each paving stone,
the light drizzle cooling my skin,

then return to the dryness of the center,
the bench warped by seasons,
and sit in the silence, remembering.

.   .

My mother's mother
digs a hole in the dirt yard
of the new tract home,
lowers the sapling
then drops to her knees
to uncomb its ball of roots.
She hums as she holds the trunk
upright, and gathers back all
that was displaced, securing
the base of the Chinese Lace Elm,
tamping the soil firm with open hands.

The Sweet Alyssum
she had carefully dug up,
roots and all, from her own
garden, and she plants it now
in a ring around the new tree,
imagining as she sings
how it all might take hold,
re-seeding every spring after
she is gone, never dreaming
her own last breath is less than
a handful of seasons away.

Three years later, another planting:
my father's father digs a hole
opposite, by the curbside post,
and sinks a limb of younger wood –
a sawed-off branch from the giant
Balm of Gilead Cottonwood in his own dirt yard
at nearly the exact longitude on a bead
due north, just past the foothills
on the other side of the San Gabriel Mountains,
crosscut and carried over the ridge,
planted like a flag trailing our colors.

.   .   .

The transplant sprouts
lime green tendrils,

thrusts new roots
into rich earth

yards beneath this blanket
of blue and white alyssum.

Massive limbs
growing thick as my torso

and heart-shaped leaves:
fluttering cottonwood blooms,

now filling the sky
like thunderheads.

I imagine my blood line

thirteen generations back –

     The woman whose eyes I share.
     The man whose curve of hand
     matches mine exact

     as he reaches out
     to cup her jaw line,
     stretches his thumb across

     to the other cheek
     to stop the fear
     before she can taste it.

     Ancestors
     migrating,
     abandoning

     soil known for generation
     after generation as
           home.

How far back does it run?
How far before the humming
can no longer reach through?

         .   .   .   .

I cup my hand around
the dry trunk of ash

close my eyes
until sleep threatens

trying to imagine
their faces

trying to follow the pulse of sap
all the way back to the taproot

envisioning the trees now
as arrows once shot to the sky

shafts of trunks returned inverted
treetop arrowheads sunken

and root cluster quills spread high
leaf palettes of green chlorophyll esters

mixed half from full-spectrum sunlight
half from the thick carbon exhalations

of the wandering mammals below
awakening beneath towering emergents

to resume
the inverted search

digging through branches
for sustenance

reaching up
to find their roots

   ·   ·   ·   ·   ·

Two million years ago
lubberly apes slumbered
in deep grasses, moonlit
sleep narratives enfolding:
clack of stones chipping
sharp shard moths.

One-hundred thousand years ago
those from the same blood
called for the sleep storytellers
to come, sang against the fear,
lit fires in the rain.

Ten thousand years ago
those who traveled to this camp
cupped awkward hands
to drink cold creek water
beside lapping dogs,
abandoned night ashes
like footprint stains
marking their journey.

The earth grows richer.
Mastodon dung and camel skin
squeeze into denser oily goo
beneath the pressure of plates.

Leaf and animal
tumble and fall,
decompose,
compress

into thick mulch,
layer after layer –
bark and marrow,
tooth and bone,

      sandstone and shale.
      Mouse scat erodes small as sand.
      The hunter's own feces mixes
      with bits of crushed tusk,

      cat skull and bison blood,
      broken beak and feather tuft.
      Human hair decomposing
      in bluish-white bird excrement.

      Mold and rot,
      fermentation and decay,
      slender chemical chains
      binding and elegant:

      all alive,
      all dancing –
      new forms swarming
      from anaerobium.

    .   .   .   .   .   .

      The shadow man

over whose bones I sit

      once slept on an oily stain under a
          full moon,
      and when he awoke dug up
          dried feces
      of a beast unknown, the rich
          black lump
      snowing a fine silt of
          ancestral smells.

When he first found this creek,
south of the wild night howling,
he dug with flint in the dirt
    a line and a peak –
big mountain –
abundance –
and buried seven singing stones
    in the soil.

After many moons and suns
    had strung
a necklace of seasons around
    his neck,
he scraped with green volcanic glass
the tanned hide that hung
    from the door of his hut –
a diamond and triangle butterfly
to signify everlasting life.

Then, with purple of crushed
    juniper berry,
salt of sweat and brick-red blood,
painted beside it an eight-spoked
    wheel –
permanence –
marking this place, north of the big
    windy river
and hemmed by two black creeks, as
    home.

.   .   .   .

I walk out

    into the garden,

smell rain

    as if a memory
    before it stings.

Off

    the path –

far from

    the dryness of new ash,
    shelter of branches,
    remembrance of white

sparks, white sky –

    the downpour begins,
    darkening the soil,
    releasing
    the collective scent
    of all whose home

this once was,

will be,

is now.

·　·　·　·　·　·

Home:
omphalos manhole cover.
The lid of a city water meter box
sunken at the edge of a lawn

serves as first base. A touch
of the fence post at the opposite curb
claims third. Second base, a stain of oil
leaked in the middle of the street

from the old family DeSoto, or perhaps
the pale yellow Helms Truck the summer before.
No pitcher's rubber or mound, just a small
        round surveyor's benchmark
bolted to the center of the cul-de-sac.

Play ball –
Sunday afternoon, 1963.
Vin Scully's tin voice
wafts down the block

from black plastic radios
on vacant work benches,
the garage doors kept open
as children play

wide eyed
until the ball
is lost against
a darkening sky.

Backyard barbecues
lift rippling heat,
lighter fluid cheers
through the cooling air,

and the world will never end,
no one ever dies –
Kennedy on the TV,
Wonder on the hi-fi,

and everyone,
even the unsuspecting child,
is safe at
            home.

.   .   .   .   .

Molten bloom
eight-hundred million years ago
and the single land mass
Pangaea rifts apart,
dividing the lone
Panthalassa ocean.

Massive plates
slide and slam
beneath the waves,
tectonic shifts
lift new continents
into starlight.

Jigsaw land masses
push off from each other
like boats from a common shore,
separating species, the ocean
thrashing to fill the great wounds

left between.

After the cooling,
after spine after spine
of newly formed ranges
emerge, a level basin settles
to form a shallow shelf
just offshore,

and a strange flat fish,
its eyes gray blisters,
glides like a silver disk
to the bottom, flutters
to cover itself safe under
a soft blanket of sandy
        loam.

.   .   .   .

leaf fall
lethal laughter of autumn
accepting the dance

first stroll
lost and risking all to
find true north

.   .   .

dream brother calls with open throat
                         the crow telling secrets on his
                             shoulder

                         kakaar
                         makaaho
                         piinor
                                 che'ee'ax

                         woshii
                         tukuut
                         toroovem
                         'akuutesh
                                 yakeenax

quail
mourning dove
hummingbird
        sing

dog
wildcat
dolphin
butterfly
        dance

                         yovaareka'

                         fourteen-pointed cog stone
                         abalone shell anointment

my father   my mother   *nenaak*   *nyook*
my hands   my bone   *nemaaman*   *ne'een*
my heart   my blood   *neshuun*   *nexaayn*
all   *'wee*

steatite pipe with bird bone stem
sucking darkness from within

earth	grass	*'ooxor*	*mamaahar*
night	moon	*yaawket*	*mwaar*
stars	sleep	*shushuu'ram*	*yataamkok*
old house		*kivaa'*	

yovaareka'

dream crawler
of a different tongue

pelt of bobcat across his back
moves through sticky mud

the secret told in water
and soil

washed free
in the cold current

releasing cloudy whispers
to the creek bottom

prayers of the hunt downstream
and the sun warming

here   *'ekwaa*

overcast	rain	*yuupet*	*'akwaaken*
water	stream	*paar*	*wenoot*
river	seashore	*paxaayt*	*'ahaavkomen paar*

open throated
answers

black arrow
brown fur stuck to the shaft
broken in mud
beside femur

covered in blankets of seasons

white arrow missed the heart
of the beast charging
whose chest flashed tan
opening closing

but this time not enfolding

whistle of white arrow feather
stroked length of spine
sunk unbroken
in the snow behind

blue arrow snapped on rock

was shot to the sky in triumph
after red arrow
found the heart
of the prey

best chert arrowhead lost

willing sacrifice

rocks eroding to river rush

charm stones thrown

       pronghorn effigies

all unseen beneath and before
contributing to the story of here

                blunt residue of night colors
                coating the hunter's mouth at dawn

my lead shaft scratching paper
wearing shorter with longer lines

                sharp taste of prey
                at back of throat

       .   .

I can sense in the tension of this pre-storm air
a vague song struggling to vibrate itself into another form,
into a shape inside my neck, my throat thickening
as I attempt to sing it to life, as if for the ages

(or as if for the angels some say exist) – as if some remnant
spirit is watching me struggle here alone, calling for the lost
child to open his mouth to the sky as it opens above him,
the song about to die in his chest, lost forever if he doesn't.

The scent of rain brings with it
the first words of a story
I had not heard before,
but now begin to taste.

My lips form a circle

to match the drops.
My mouth shapes a chamber
for what is emerging

but only single syllables come,
mimicking the distinct
sound of each fall:
staw... puct... stuh...

I sense no words,
but can taste
in their shape
a vague new awareness.

                    Forty thousand years ago
                    clouds of hands stained smoky caves
                    and hunters migrated
                    ice-free corridors.

                    Six thousand years ago
                    blunt reeds pressed
                    old stories deep
                    into weeping clay.

The tales my ancestors told
were far away and foreign,
of soil I have not walked,
scents I have not known.

My parents' blood was already
a mixture before they embraced.
I have inherited
only fragments of stone.

I can only imagine the odd skeletons
buried long before my arrival,
the mingled slough of stories and seasons,

shed from trees and plants,

insects and beasts, clans that walked
across a strait long since submerged,
distant campfires left behind,
flickering like dim stars.

.

On the outskirts of a supercluster
    of galaxies,
a score of milky spirals are bound
by one another's pull.

In the distant suburbs of one of
    the swirls,
one medium-sized star spins
in a remote arm-spray of stars –

and a hurtling stone
ricochets off of a new planet
burbling gases into blue.

Constellations strewn across
ridiculous darkness
remind, in turn,
        of distant campfires.

Faint light that ancient stars
        emitted eons ago
and the newer glow of nearby suns
arrive on my cones and rods simultaneously.

And everything here
is merely the same
simple star ash rearranged.

Could it be that all is present,
that everywhere is contained
in where we are?

                              Pregnant mother mammal
                              squatting,
                              her child echoing the cries

                              of the dance
                              months before
                              when seed was planted in thrust.

I rise and walk along the picket fence,
recalling how I once dragged toy trucks across this ground,
mounded dirt with smaller hands, filled plastic pails
with earthwormed soil, wondering how deep I could go.

A few seasons back I measured and hammered pine stakes,
found my plumb line, tied yellow string taut and slammed
cranky-hinged post-hole diggers straight down and deep,
slicing through the strata of past seasons stacked below,

raising new blisters and questions, prying lines of root
and tendrils from throaty soil, rich textures rising as
I raised a fence along the perimeter and claimed this yard
        as possession –
but I am beginning to sense the short-sightedness
        of such endeavors.

This neighborhood was one fenceless, yes, but long before
        that it was ocean floor,
then heaved up to become swampy shore, then river bottom,
then fields that were farmed and plowed and paved over,

and as a child I ran around this street as if it were a field

and crawled on my belly and scraped and squinted at
      the constellations in the crevices.
All of it humming – all of it – teeming with life:
spirochetes swarming wild on black asphalt, saprophytes
      thriving on dead matter,
bacteria and aphid, flowering molds, rusts and smuts.

I ache to return to that place of no distinctions,
beyond differentiation. Not my yard opposite others,
or garden against concrete, language against chaos, or
home against wild – but *all*, and *all wild.*

A strange new yet familiar hunger is calling me
to look deeper in and farther back, stand as one of the ones
transplanted and learn to read the music written on the staves
of this slipping Pacific Plate onto which I was born,

plant a pole vertically into this place
as *axis mundi* – find the downbeat
beyond the heartbeat of here and now
and plunge deep into the reiterating hum.

I want to claim the greater rhythms
of underground rivers connecting,
babble in a tongue that does not distinguish
between *home* and *all, stuh* and *one.*

I need to drop to my knees,
break the earth with my hands,
dig for smooth stones
once seen in floating dreams.

ii.

(Blue Shadows:
Starlight Bath)

~

what is significant:
a sill with no window

the coldness of a key
to the lock of a house
    now burned to the ground

blue fields
of the one left alone

moonlight
mistaken for spilled milk

red rim of rock
mocking

the splintered wood color
in a torn branch above

white flash of eye
and the retraction of love

oozing
dark ink

black arrow that misses
sunken shaft growing roots

hunt for food uncovering
stiff flint leaves

abalone fishhooks
olivella and acorn shells

black asphaltum-held
feather fletching

fluted sides
     of clovis

                    fear transformed
                    into adrenaline

                    face to face
                    with the beast

                    clack of tooth
                    on tooth

                    the nose torn
                    to ragged flaps

The dreamlike
compression of time

               beating of featherless limbs
               mimicking slow-motion propulsions

               in the transition from liquid sac
               to pneumatic lung

               all that came before
               forgotten

               for one chance
               to breath the sky

               plugs between worlds
               sucked free

               by the basting plunger
               of Lethe

                         rack of hand

                    relaxes from fist

rain bead
in curled petal reflects

nectar specked
with bee dung

              an unlocked door
                        a home

                        forever open
                        to the sky

                    ~   ~

              jacks like stars
              hurl through space

              lock into clusters
              on the plane of the porch

              awkward constellations
              of tri-axial suns

              bounce one-sie two-sie
              or hop on one foot

              across hopscotch boxes
              drawn in chalk

              on concrete sidewalks
              a bead-chain lager toss

and a wobbling bend
a dangling limb reaching

~   ~   ~

It was the purple grace of Sweet Alyssum
that defined the placement of the path.
My brain insisted one way, arguing
in eloquence of Euclidean logic
for a straight course between
the porch and the gate. But the heart
(never good at logic or direction)
demanded something else:

respect for things encountered
along the way, regardless of
distance or convenience.
And so I succumbed,
laying pink paving stones
in a snaking trail to avoid.
Perhaps more than required,
but no more than necessary.

And now, like Aeneas moaning on his knees
struggling to uproot a shrub of myrtle,
I plant my foot, lean back
straight-armed against a weed between pavers
and hear the earth groan in resistance.
Why are such distinctions made?
Blue and white alyssum preferred
over bluegrass and dandelion?

Diamond over limestone's gray?
Plutonic granitic magma stacks over
phyllite's wavy greenish sheen? Or
hard quartzite mines over cliffs of clay?
I spend the rest of the day digging
blue-black dirt from under nails,
smell of myself mingling
                    with the hunter before me:

                              song of the whales
                              swimming this sky
                              (or the space this sky was
                              before the slide of the planet)
                              the birth of the calf
                              thirty-three million years ago
                              and the sport of breath
                              released above water line.

Now it is desert.
Now the sea has receded,
glaciers have come and gone,
come and gone. Now we walk
ocean floors exposed to star heat direct,
and I am left in an untended garden
here in this pale bath of starlight,
this low level hum –

radio radiation
from when the mass of light
finally burst apart from the pull of the core.
I stand looking up at the stars casting their glow,
throwing ghost shadows of my form
in every direction around me,
too faint and violet to discern,
yet part of the odd stories missed.

In the morning I repeat the pose,

head back, but those same suns
have now disappeared, lost behind
morning's brilliant dome, forgotten
for the time being. The lizard witness
on the wall, straight-lipped and still,
seeks only the heat of the new day
and the memory of yesterday's sun on brick.

Tonight I will lie with the ache
of today's futile gardening
still thrumming in my limbs,
the earth hardening under my nails –
dirt grit on tooth enamel,
the smell of a singular past
still stinging and congealing
in the corners of my eyes.

~   ~   ~   ~

the fruit on the vine
did not ask to be planted
and so it fell

                the water wheel turns
                and scoops
                the unsuspecting water

                        rivers wind down
                        from mountains
                        eroding

fruits
bruise

                        the rains do not fall
                        they fly

salt
lifted off white desert

carried
on dry currents

stings the cheek
becomes part of the breath

Santa Ana sands on hot wind
the silicate on skin –

vision alone
is not enough

to distinguish
the difference

              ~   ~   ~   ~   ~

              The Balm of Gilead dreams its memory:
              blasting heat, dry rocky soil,
              families of stones surrounding.

              But *genus populus* grows
              only one sex, relying on the differences
              of others nearby, the wild incest of groves.

              Hermaphrodite elm flowers, samara keys of seeds

encased in papery wings, spin like helicopters
in the breeze, but find no root to hold.

The transplant stands alone in the corner
unable to reproduce – basal shoot reasoning.
The three trees sharing this garden floor

tangle their roots into one dense tapestry,
lift ridges across the yard like the veins
on the back of my hand. Their canopies

spread unpruned, fight each other for daylight,
are freshened only by the rain.
Inverted arrows; willing sacrifices.

The immediacy of such strange soil.
Thirty-nine summers in a place without seasons –
August seemed a lifetime, and I'm still in it.

~   ~   ~   ~   ~   ~

The evergreen stands in deciduous dreams
as I feel no seasons passing in my bones.

Undefined stimulus to shed leaves
as I imagine the weight of immortality:

persistence of plots and excavations,
upending imbroglios of pericarps and stones.

The warmth of blooms on stem haunts the bark
as that innermost spongy pith displaces my breath.

What does it matter? So long as our gestures
carry the grace of the curve of the earth,

so long as the breeze finds us all
without judgment, and the seasons pass

forgivingly, in shade or sunlight,
over each of us as we slumber.

~   ~   ~   ~   ~   ~   ~

I ease myself down
into the old yellow tub

filling with hot water
in scent of wax and steam

a candle at both ends
burning at head and feet

thirteen years
it's been since I've bathed here

I calmly observe
my soft flesh

white scars
hair swaying

like swamp grasses
slow motion underwater

candle skipping sparks

like stones across the surface

water splashes and slaps
answer off the glass

soaking out the tinge
of the day's toil

I move my foot along
the bottom of the tub

and the shell
cries

aching at such naked
human touch

there's the rub
of this world

hollow yellow
filled with warm fluid

two-thirds saline
solution

pulled by a moon

                              that once glanced here

stiff joints in a
steaming bath

              warm water sac
              wrapping skin

a womb of
concentric shells

light behind flesh
in a tub between tiles

within walls of a home
under a dome of sky

the sun and moon
dragging the tides

fingertip whorls wrinkled
from extended submersion

it is

enough

I shall be
rising soon

I have spent too long in this place
where too much ends in precipitation

and is too easily
forgotten

house creaks
and thick shell squeals

underwater echoes
as eardrums submerge

    and a lone whale
    its breath almost spent

    sings a last song before surfacing
    in the shallow water just offshore

I remain still
become aware of enfolding silence

strain to hear more
of the spatial symphony

two rooms away
Pärt's *Passio*

on the stereo
so sparse

I can not tell
the song from the caesura

listen

        listen

a momentary moaning of cellos

no

a car pulling away

distant intersection
unseen traveler

solo pilot
slicing through clouds

a single oboe's
low reverberations

a moan
more than a note

long wet reeds creaking
like goose wing in swamp

the cough from old windows
rattling loose in the pane

my vision has grown blurry
after nearly   thirty-nine years

this house and I
are the same age

but its studs   existed
                  hidden in trees

                  long before they were felled and sawn
                  hauled and measured

                  re-sawn and nailed
                  to stand erect

once again
in this place

their rings   trapping isotopes of carbon and oxygen
                gulps of sky that testify to each specific season

earlier in the day I wrapped my hand
around the trunk of the elm

                  like I did as a child
the diameter now three times as thick

and realized that same old trunk
                still exists

encased within
concentric growth rings

I imagine my hand
                proportionately smaller as well

the ghost of itself in the space now filled
with the solidified residue

                from seasons
                of emergence

dead heart wood
most of the weight

alive only in the thin skin
of bark phloem and xylem

I fall deeper into the silence
awaiting the next movement

straining to hear
strings emerging

or the *blum*
of a kettledrum struck once

the silence between
containing all somehow

smell of wick
smoke signals

smell of myself

exfoliating

peeled bark
smooth beneath

new skin sebum
after a shed scab

walls beading moisture
on the other side unseen

like thick flesh
wet and rubbery inside

slickness of the balloon
fragile bag taut between tensions

pressure from within
out

pressure from without
in

stiffening the skin
like a canvas sail bloomed full

the ringing in my ears
masking more silence beyond

I become aware there is a hum
from the old house herself

like an antique refrigerator
clunking to life and rattling pans

the tub a diaphragm
vibrating

the length of my being
pressed hard against

I can feel the studs creak involuntarily
from slow push of roots below

reluctantly relinquishing
the bind of nail in wood

bolts twisting back
down the threads

one click at a time
once per season

joist sag and plaster crack
my soaking joints click and creak

too still for too long
only the subtle nudgings within

the settling goes unnoticed
compromises accepted unawares

the earth shifts and
things are displaced despite

~   ~   ~   ~   ~   ~

bird wings beat down gusts
fluttering leaves
in the cold air above the roof

midnight migrations through dark skies

the air thinning until
                beyond the shell
                of water and carbon
                                spinning suns streak across the void

                                their planets spinning madly
                                    along with them
                                sliding as one across the darkness
                                rotating in turn as part
                                of a glowing galaxy of suns

                                the galaxies in turn clustering
                                together as if one larger sun
                                and these clusters clumping
                                    as superclusters
                                strung as lacy webs of filaments

                                flowing and dividing like watershed
                                in a vast cosmic network
                                connecting immeasurable heavens
                                our local Laniakea spraying radiation

                                moving as one
                                in a universe
                                that is itself whirling
                                and blooming outward

                                self-similar fractals at every scale
                                each thing defined
                                    by every other thing
                                consciousness sparking
                                at every seam of entity

whorled fingertips
submerge

to pull the plug free
and the swirling suds spiral

naked in front of the mirror
whose glass has held my form like a lover
the silver back echoing back to me
moment by moment the finest of details

the small but sudden growings
of my life
the slow and larger lives
of my growing

the walls and studs
the hardwood floors
        cured through years
        by the vibrations of my voice

I flop damp and naked onto cool sheets
and listen for movements I might have missed
a jet somewhere screaming through clouds unseen
trailing swirls of heat through mist

the clouds themselves spiral galaxies
as seen from the cockpit
of the jet draining
into an eye of vortex

reflecting off ears' timpani
through black windows
and back into the sky
lowering in pitch

descending with the first fall
of unexpected rain
softer and farther still until
just a rumble fading

~   ~   ~   ~   ~

I fall into restless sleep
into a memory
of   stepping forward

            holding my weight
            suspended for one heartbeat
            on the ball of my foot

            and a burn flashes
            up the back
            of my leg

as when earlier in the day
I extended my stride
to reach the paving stone off the path

            or when as a child
            hopped into the box
            marked one for sorrow

            snowy image
            of Neil Armstrong
            in weak blue glow

wet footprint
on a round rug
in front of the tub

            a stiff flag saluted
            on a strange horizon

the shadow the same

and the widow still grieving
and the men to blame
nod and turn away

rockets ripping darkness
into light
and dust

preachers
and madmen
screaming of the end

a duck-and-cover drill
nape of neck bent too far
tight and aching

curved ridge of spine
brushing gum
stuck

hands clasped
tight at back of skull
and windows slammed shut

as if glass or eyes
are expected to survive
if the class melds into
        bony racks

~   ~   ~   ~

the bird-bone whistler
played through here

strung a bow of hair
left his drum in sunlight

beside last night's memory
of flame

recalled the dream of
flash and rattle

smeared gray ash
across his forehead

across the scar on his nose
remembrance of the smell

of common blood
before the hunt

pressed thumbs
over closed eyelids

to mark the stain
he cannot see himself

but through which
his clan can see

their own grace
and stumblings in him

all striving to find
the common ground where

stars

become fathers' eyes

shell of sky
becomes ancestor breath

earth
the heartbeat manifest

underground rivers merging
and blood yet blended

we don
the common mask

begin
the shared song of the hunt

draw
the string taut

close
our eyes

and dive
into the sound of the drum

~   ~   ~

I have walked in circles
along the red brick planter
ringing a single orange tree
lone survivor of the excavated grove

tight-roped across the browns and greens
of a braided rug
on the hardwood floor
of the new family home

leapt across the planter of stones
on the desert homestead
surrounding the parent cottonwood
its limbs sawn smooth and pale

I've played naked in the Mojave sun
re-rerouted water across the sand and patted
    mud dams
fired rocks at yucca stalk strike zones
and gazed at the measureless open horizon

walked out toward unknown regions
felt myself floating above ripples of
    unseen rivers
looked up in perfect silence
at the ridiculous canopies of stars

I have read the twisted longhand
of a windmill's folded A-frame
pulled down by unknown vandals
rewriting innocence to incomprehension

I have witnessed the signature of rattler
scrawled in sand
chased quail and jackrabbit
over ridge roads

seen the silhouettes of loved ones
disappearing without goodbyes
faint mirages of silver and blue ribbons
rippling in the distance

I have walked along
this river before
under a clay-faced
    moon

I have gone nowhere in the time between
held in orbit
counting futile laps
around a dying star

I have swept the brown paper skins
of old cocoons off of eaves
as a solitary butterfly witness
tumbles from the tree

lights upon the gate post
in the darkening yard
folds its orange wings straight up together
as if hands in some insect prayer

sad ceremony
slow motion sweeping
    long flights
    to barren seas

    Cronkite's voice buzzes
    through the front door screen.

    From the open door of the garage
    an unattended radio crackles

    as Vin Scully talks a different
    round rock home:

    . . . good breaking ball snakes its way
    through the zone for a strike.

Well, I hope you're all comfortable
and things are okay where you are –

popped way up, and I mean way,
way up . . .

~   ~

In dreams I wander this house
checking doors and windows

endlessly in the same routine
forgetting what had come before

daylight breathing has found me unaware
tracing the same steps as in sleep

a mindless wandering
down hallways

perpetually orbiting
rooms

checking
again and again

the same locks
in the same order

passing through thresholds
without recognition

my wrist twisting against

brass resistance

never registering
or accepting the fact

things are as safe
as they will ever be

nothing
not even the creation

in sleep
can stop

the ice cold unknown
just beyond the tumblers

on the other side
of the glass

~

tin can on asphalt rasp
I awaken with a gasp
unsure of the hour

the soft light bleeds
around the blinds drawn
disguising the angle of the sun

I turn away
my mouth ringing with sleep acids

the sharp bite aftertaste of
wine from a metal cup

behind the blinds
a square of dusk
hangs

all colors have diffused
in the time I was away
all is cast with a sickly gray

and I am still
unsure of the time

of what has passed
unnoticed

the room is flooded
with a thick stillness
the heavy grip of dream residue

as somewhere outside
a dove mocks the distant chant
of an empty tin can

kicked across asphalt
skidding and rattling

beyond the step
of a child

iii.

(Maps and Legends:
History and Wilderness)

∞

I sit down

    in the map room,

smell stale dust –

     as if cells
     of dead skin.

On

    the shelves,

in flat files

     built of sanded ash,
     large sheets stacked
     by region.

Parks, dark roads –

     the search now begins
     to find the soil
     within ink.
     Representative lines
     that mark the home

once found, shared,

then lost

somehow.

∞   ∞

Two maps,
identical.

Both legends
read the same:

"Prepared under the direction of
the Chief of Engineers, U.S. Army, 1942."

Only one bears the title: "War Department"
and a red stamp: "Restricted – Grid Zone G."

My father just thirteen,
the whole world at war

when this map
was issued,

detailing wells,
accessible roads,

future homes,
ink as soil.

*NOTE: Officers
using this map*

*will mark hereon
corrections and additions*

*which come to their attention
and mail direct to...*

For thirteen hours

I remain in the library

curled over maps
spread across tables

like homestead grids
seen from an airplane

tracing my finger over
            dash-line gravel roads

                dit-and-dah Morse code
                river beds

                            forgotten creeks
                no longer evident

for the newer seasons'
layers of pavement

                aerial photographs
                reducing roof and curb

                to flea egg flecks
                and eyelash shadows

                Thomas Brothers'
                blacks and oranges

                the green-line contour intervals
                of geologic surveys

                resource water tables
                vertical geodetic data

                Abel Stearns' Rancheros
                Las Bolsas flatlands

haciendas
missions

new homes built

                 on sacred grounds

            konaashnga
            koshiiy

            tayiiy honuuka'
            'wee 'eyoohiinkem

weather maps reveal off shore gusts
that follow the path of the ancient river inland

even though
the river is gone

west winds billow
my curtains inward

blow straight through
this house

convection currents over yards built over old river bottom
          that became river bottom again

          some eighty years ago
          when the rains lasted days and

          the Santa Ana River raged and
          swelled and flooded her banks

          flooded the undeveloped land
          flooded again just twenty-two years later

                    flooded streets and houses and
                    orchard after orchard of Valencia oranges

I swear I can smell it all
as I tap my nail on the key

this frostless zone
so prone to overflowing

                    ∞   ∞   ∞

Thirteen days later
I fly north, as if in migration.

Son of a pilot
but new to such perspective,

I study the swath of coastline,
the three-plumed wakes of boats far below.

I imagine a similar shape of contrail vortices
trailing behind us through the wispy cirrus,

the history of this journey quickly written
then disappearing, water vapor

deposition and sublimation,
like   the condensation and evaporation

                              of migration songs sung
                              in the chill of a desert night,

                              quick clouds of breath

                    rising into darkness and forgotten.

Banking back inland, climbing,
I can't distinguish the difference

between road
and arroyo,

fold and freeway,
fault and firebreak,

the transition from garden to field,
ear pop to revelation.

Bighorn sheep bound over
sagebrush and scree,

boulder to boulder,
crossing the San Gabriel Mountains.

Here it is. The raw land
my father's father saw at my age

as he gazed north from the foothills
out into the baking Mojave,

his back turned to the range
and the ocean beyond with its

                    secret deep mountains
                    and prehistoric fish

                    gliding like birds
                    between exotic peaks in a denser sky.

∞   ∞   ∞   ∞

when I was thirteen
I chained my bedroom door from the inside
left a note on my pillow that I was "out for a walk"

slipped the screen from the casement window
and climbed quietly out of my family's new home
into the still August night

I trotted down the hill
walked through the tract streets
named for places far away that I had never seen

and wandered down to the concrete ravine
three miles away to seek the course of the river
approaching from the other side

> where coyote howl
> once curved the night
> like the waters themselves

I followed its flat bed
between concrete banks
rising on either side like wings

to the place where the walls
steepened and narrowed
and a feeder conduit five feet across

pierced through the sloping wall
the source behind its black circle opening
unknown

I lowered my head as if in respect

and stepped inside the concrete pipe's
dark circumference

each breath and step echoed
with water trickles
the darkness dank and thick

no room to stand
I remained bent forward
as if falling into each new step

leaning into the future
with no expectation
other than to risk and step out

and see where it led me
a rite of passage I can see now
a test to prove myself

I spread the width of each stride
to land along the curve of wall
above the water line

ankles and groin aching
as I trudged its snaking route
beneath the streets

deep enough that the sound
from rumbling trucks overhead
could not reach through

under a vacant lot then
under a schoolyard's
swing sets and playground

under a little league field
its wooden snack bar

padlocked and empty

under palm trees with shallow roots
under magnolias with their pre-bee tepals
and ancient ivory flowers

under a radio transmission tower
under telephone poles
under tract homes

with dark bedrooms
where other clans slept
suspended above me

sprawled like battlefield dead
unaware of how their daily gestures
and suburban jetsam

might one day meld
into the odd strata of journeys
accumulating beneath them

I plodded secretly onward
an awkward blind mole
stumbling underground

distances unknown
shoulders slumped to match
the arc of the pipe's diameter

a staggering step at a time
my bent spine on fire
not knowing where it was leading

not knowing where I was
losing track of true north
from all the bends

unknowingly following
        a young woman's footprints
        once made in deep mud

        following creek beds
        carrying her child
        to the Council Tree

our footfalls   lacing now
odd dance   partners in perfect step but for
centuries   between

but for the Portland cement
binding sand aggregate and granite
into this fallopian drainpipe cocoon

        imaginal buds transforming

unsure if my eyes were open
or closed in the carbon blackness
losing track of all time

        to the point of no time

convergence of place
across an unlighted Noh play stage
simultaneity and singularity

        beyond differentiation

I thought   (or dreamt in my waking state)
that I was seeing sparks
          as the blind see "phantom light"

          or an amputee
          feels an itch in the limb
          no longer attached

          synapses to the missed past

          a downed power line flailing

          internal chaos snapping
          orange and blue sparks
          glint of copper through black

          the snake sliced clean in two
          by a *schlunk* of shovel blade
          whips its cursive memory of wholeness

          to curl
          back upon
          itself

I stopped and touched my fingertips
to the bridge of my nose
my eyes burning

I pressed my lids
until checkerboard black-and-white
patterns danced and fluttered

          like the palimpsest
          erased from a lifescript of skin twitches
                    faint echoes of double helix
                    muscle memory from forefathers
                    and foremothers stored dormant

for centuries in a chain of DNA
inherited then released in common
        gestures:

a sidelong glance at news of sorrow
echoed sklent
in the great-great-grandson
the akimbo pose
with a cracking of thumb joint
        on hip bone
done the same
by the fourteenth mother back

the idle roaming of tip of tongue
to explore the narrow ridges
        on the back of the teeth
and the palatine raphe
        on the roof of the mouth
just as the common mother
rocking with eyes closed
thirty-six million sunsets ago
taught us all

and we stumble ahead
unaware of the sources of our grace
from whence or from whom
what similar shapes once displaced the sky
as the sheets slept on night after night
inherit folds
ironed sharp by the dead weight
    of those asleep

plane after plane
consonantal remnants furrowed
creases that lace this history
ghosts of lines once stained
erasure yielding the clear impression

      of what was written here before
subtle as the web of wrinkles
netting each knuckle

       dried river and delta fan
flux of hand repeating
palm whorl manuscripts
in crows-feet meters
rerouted trails
still extant
in relief

not better

necessarily

   abandoned

   epidermal white
     of shed conception

   scraped parchment cicatrix
smooth skin of rubbed vellum
and veins fading
under rubbery cover
etched relief
whispering traces of the stories
behind us and under us

once the repetition of my footfalls
became a meaningless ring
like a familiar word repeated to nonsense

a blade of light appeared
plunging diagonally
across the nothingness ahead

I quickened my staggering gait toward it
my thoughts re-gaining shape
surfacing as if from deep underwater

my chest flooded warm
with the thought of miasma mist
exhaled into the open night

darkness expunged
and the re-filling of lungs
with morning

when I got to the wedge of light
slanting in as if from a Vermeer window
I saw it was a steep conduit jutting forty-five degrees

a hollow arm reaching in
from the other side
as if to save me

I extended my arms up
and into the narrow chute
wedged my shoulders against its sides

kicked myself up off of the floor
my ribs supporting my entire weight
wet shoes suspended midair

halfway in

halfway out

I wriggled
my heavy form
up toward freedom

and emerged finally

into a shallow sloping chamber
with a thick steel plate as lid
flush with the street
at the seam of the curb

I rolled onto my back
and pushed with bunched legs
until the heavy plate
squawked its submission and swung aside
revealing a cobalt blue sky

I rocked to my feet
and slowly uncurled
clicking my spine
straight again
an exhausted sob choking free

pant legs soaked
from the storm-drain soup
of lawn sprinkler runoff
and the piss and excrement
of rats, birds, and homeless

in the diffused light of pre-dawn
my wet shirt clinging to my spine
tail lights streaked past
as nauseating wakes of diesel fuel clouds
gusted into my face

from *whoosh* after *whoosh* of passing travelers

when I saw the radio transmission tower
I realized my bearings:

I was facing Los Angeles
unseen in the distance

my home was behind me

I was standing on the arterial road
paralleling the Santa Ana freeway

only a few hundred yards
from Coyote Creek

on the other side of the sooty chain-link

just a few yards from my face
cars and trucks roared past

each unaware of my journey
each rumbling their unknown loads

toward Ursa Minor

∞   ∞   ∞   ∞   ∞

Some nine-thousand nights later
I drive back home, southbound on the 5 Freeway,
sailing over v-shaped seams of rock
locked silent and dry beneath the pavement.

As I *whoosh* past the radio transmission tower

the scent of that night spent walking the storm drain
stirs a twinge in my back – the same ache as decades later
when I hunched for hours over the musty maps
and memorized the names of these feeder creeks and channels.

I nod and take the exit near the place where I had resurfaced

and zigzag the route of Coyote Creek
via surface streets,
left and right turns
through the quiet neighborhoods

past other clans asleep in dark bedrooms.

I slowly roll past familiar looking tract homes
with corner fence posts and sloping eaves,
roll over oily stains in the middle of streets
where children still imagine fields,

and I superimpose the swampy grasslands that were here before.

My car follows the tributary's diagonal route southwest
until it joins the San Gabriel River,
and I gaze south to where it finds the sea
at the bay called *Alamitos*: "little cottonwoods."

And at last I can see her: the woman walking home with her child
    beside the river, in a bath of moonlight, singing to remember.

When I finally arrive home I sit silent in the driveway
staring at Polaris until daybreak, watching the violet crown
of dawn re-inhabit the sky, displacing the night, knowing now
the transitions from old watersheds to here.

∞   ∞   ∞   ∞   ∞   ∞

The new day brings with it
fresh perspectives as I begin
trimming bushes and sawing limbs,

light flooding in on soil
too long in the shade.

Some plants reject grafts too alien
to the native rootstock, and I will not
attempt to appropriate cultures and
customs beyond my reach
and understanding.

I will not romanticize the past.
The muddy dark holds shell after shell
of unworthy myths, and perhaps I've sunk
yet another with this, but there will
always be some leaking boat
left behind as new revelations arrive.

I cannot deny the mistakes I've made.
I will not raise my hand to the breaking waves
and ask them to stop. We are all
rightful inheritors, worthy of shared
reciprocity, the interdependence of our histories
and futures remain woven inextricably together.

My dogs crisscross the yard excitedly,
noses to the soil, reminding of scents and stories
still beyond my reach, but connected nevertheless.
Each new planting by each new resident –
beginning with the first to arrive and continuing
ever since – was part of this shared hope.

This stretch of earth has become
a chaotic basin of displacement
                constructed by immigrant laborers
                who planted fence posts like flagpoles,
                mistaking residence for ownership,
                reshaping the landscape in their own image
                    of paradise.

Myopic gardeners instead of careful guardians.
Dominion by exploitation in the place of
    stewardship.
Unjust enrichment with no recompense
    and enslavement
in the name of gods unknown.
Sacred grounds sold as rancheros,
fences strung to divide.

Uprooted in turn by more invaders
assuming entitlement and privilege.
Railroads pushing unbroken lines
    of new arrivals,
each replacing myth with amnesia.
Treaties breached and maps redrawn.
Abandonment of roots and legends
    for the final settlement.

        Seventy thousand years ago
        a species first ventures out of its
           homeland.

        Thirteen thousand years ago
        hunter-gatherers tame grains
          and pulse legumes,
        settling in as the seasons
          turn dryer.

Six hundred years ago the rains abandon this
golden basin. Decades later, when the currents
finally crawl back to life, from the dank silt
near the western bank of the Los Angeles River,
a sycamore grove, of all things, emerges,
thickens, spreads into a massive riparian forest,
mirroring the constant growth of immigrants
covering the open spaces to her east. One

lime-green tip pierces the alluvial soil and sends something through herself back down into the ground, as if a shudder from full-spectrum knowledge, a hum in empathy – the way a piano wire farther down the harp will begin to sing a new note off of a neighbor's vibration, resonating its own tension, augmenting the other. The sense of something deeper that needs to be charged back to life perhaps, and perhaps she could sense it, sense the power of this place and all it held before, sensed the need to tap into it and bring what came before back into the daylight, mirror perhaps the lines of ancient foot paths and creek beds in her leaf veins, a living covenant to everything that once inhabited this place, and so she surged upward to tower above all. The forest thrived in the great flood plain, even as heavy rains transformed saturated banks into new river bottom, even as currents shifted and the river re-routed itself downhill in finding the sea. Successive flash floods swept entire trees from the mud, carried them for miles, buried them under yards of sediment, but one remained unmoved, twenty-two feet around and one hundred-twenty feet high, her limbs chording the histories of the seasons in the sky.

The People of the Earth, the Indigenous People of the Brush Houses who themselves had been sung and danced into being, understood what she carried in her rising and survival, and so journeyed to her from distant villages, gathered under her canopy for ritual and counsel. Here in the Place of the Poison Oak, this one sacred sycamore threw enough shade for all. Standing shoulder to shoulder under her immense branches, the Beautiful People, Those Covered Ones, Those With the Long Arms, turned to bow to the Four Sacred Mountains – *Ywaat, 'Akwaanga, Yamiwu, Har'wovet* (Baldy, San Gorgonio, San Jacinto, Saddleback). They danced across her roots, calling the names of the Four Sacred Rivers – *Paayme Paxaayt, Chinuuy Paxaayt, Totootanga Paxaayt, Kahoo' Paxaayt* (Los Angeles River, Rio Hondo, San Gabriel River, Santa Ana River). A stream of brothers and sisters pooled together into a dancing spiral two hundred feet across, yet all were contained in the throw of her shade. Here at the center, different threads wove into the one shared story. Here, at the heart, the breaths all came from the same singing place. Here, the smell of the earth at dusk was recognized as being the same of home, no matter how long a walk away that was. "The Home at the Entrance" – *Pakooynga*. "Place of the Old Woman" – *Tuhuunga*. "Place of the Grandmother" – *'Ashuukshanga*. The home that is *Yaanga, Povuu'nga, Lukuupanga, Xaaxamonga*. The home that is *Mayoonga, Kawee'nga, Kuukamonga, Topaa'nga*. The Singer of Dreams from *Hotuuknga*, whose ashes would be scattered in the place where Sweet Alyssum would grow over his head, would compose songs to the tree's beauty for the full day's walk to her. Migrating flocks used her massive crown as reference as they approached, then flapped past unheard, overhead. Land animals drew a bead on her odd shape from distant mountains and stared, sensing something moving in her stillness. Children whispered secrets into her bark as they hugged her, the sister of all in this place where the sun finds rest, the gift of the seven giants who brought peace to the chaotic world by resting it on their shoulders.

But relentless waves of new arrivals crowded in, imposed their own names and borders, covered old roots with new bricks. They sawed away limb after limb of this Council Tree to make room for walls and massive vats of wine. On three separate winters they hacked at her heartwood and burned off her top, trying to finish her, yet each time she bloomed anew. Year after year they hewed away more and more until she lost too much foliage to sustain her massive size, and one spring her leaves simply failed to re-sprout. On her 500th birthday, the man who bought the land that contained her, who ran his business from the building that covered her largest roots, shook is head and decreed it: "She has to go." The city's best axe-man was hired. The newspaper reported it on page nine. Hundreds migrated across the southland to meet in her shade one last time, but the tribal elders were forced to the back of the crowd, their songs not allowed to disrupt the spectacle. At one point the lumberjack, removing his sweat-soaked shirt, handed his axe to a man in the front row, and the man ran forward and buried the blade with a yelp as the crowd cheered. Others then stepped up, taking turns, the people shouting as the thumps shook the bones of their feet. It took three full days to take her down. Afterward, wood chips were picked up gently, as if ripe fruit that had fallen as a gift, and gathered as mementos in pockets and purses of the witnesses, and in this way her remains were scattered across the fading tribal lands, then spread farther out over the years, slowly across the state, then the country, her presence radiating and thinning as if bits of starlight. A chip of golden sun remains in a dresser drawer in Alameda. A thin curled strip sits in a yellowed envelope stuck to the wax backing of a photo album in Hartford, no one in the family knowing what *"El Aliso"* scrawled on the front refers to. A chunk like a die rests in the pocket of a suit jacket in a sealed box buried on a hilltop in upstate New York, forgotten. Wood no longer tree, the time of unity lost, but something more than mere trivia or debris – that sunlight once transformed into solid form is something.

These are not just faceless tales of a sacred tree or a sister who walked the river before me. These are echoes of the common, forgotten. The double helix tattoo spun from the first mother and echoed extant in every mother since. Alive in a mother named Bengta, alive in 1604, passed in eye glints to survive this evening in me, and that very blood, though mixed, carries the pulse to my wrists. All of them, all of it, here with me now. Remembered by name or not, I can sense them. The man whose voice resonated like mine seventy-seven generations back, who grieved his wife's death with the same choked sob that has left my throat tonight. The mother one hundred births back, who drew her child's face near to her own and whispered, "I am honored to share this place of shadows with you," in a tongue I could not know, yet carried what has become a part of my blood too, and all of their singing has brought me to this place, mingled into this, my essence, and yes – that same prayer to the spark that she offered her child still resonates in me, in deference, and back to all of them.

∞   ∞   ∞   ∞   ∞   ∞   ∞

a few thousand feet east of
a perfect bead to magnetic north
beyond the mountains forty-two miles away
my father's father paced off long strides
equaling three feet each in balance
side-stepped foothill yucca, cottonwood,
Joshua tree and juniper
drove handmade wooden stakes
into arid foothills
seeking only to define

I too have inherited such desires
longing to claim one place as my own
to establish new thresholds
crests and colors
aching to hold this clay
for as long as I can

just as the father taught his children
how to measure each stride
how to walk in patience
with strength and confidence
in tune with the energies
humming beneath and above

in turn his son drove his own stakes
took his own children out into the yard
paced a path around the central tree
and together maintained the continuum
the father teaching by example
how to be aware
how to reach with each step and feel
as one footfall lands short
some pull inside
an inner sense

to let the next stride reach
that extra distance missed
to plant it farther
to balance
as we do
or try to do
all our lives
for others when they fall short

a zigzag
sole print
in hot sand
patterns
of diamonds
and snakes of half diamonds
                    the same design
                    the singing woman drew
                    on the rock
                    thirty-nine generations
                    directly below

when the light-skinned geologists
walked out into the desert to squint
through bright yellow sextants
and establish coordinates for future maps

balancing a bubble in fluorescein-green
to a line level with the skin of the sea
unseen beyond the Gabriels

unspooling long and narrow strips of cloth
marked meticulously to the millimeter

unaware of the hash marks on antelope hide
and decaying strips of baskets inearthed
several feet beneath them

they arrived at the places
my grandfather had marked
relying only on his instinct
balanced between lines of reason
and the innate ability
to feel when the step
toward sunlight
is right

and the men in hardhats pulled up stake after stake
replaced his markers with shiny steel embossed
with numbers and codes
sank their long spikes of progress
into the wilderness
into perfect alignment with the
                    sheath-shaped graves below:
                    skull beneath arrowhead
                    beneath feather
                    beneath stone

∞   ∞   ∞   ∞   ∞   ∞

seven thousand feet east
of the one-hundred-eighteenth parallel
a water tank sits fenced safe within
the dirt back yard of a new tract home
a communal well established to provide
the neighborhood with clean water

long before that coordinate was cross-haired
at thirty-three point eight-two-four-four degrees
     latitude
the orange grove leveled

                foundation poured
                the shell of this house raised
                and the cul-de-sac paved

                        a biomass of bacteria swarmed
                        dinosaurs and insects spread
                        sea grasses and stinging nettle
                        fused-boned ankylosauridae
                        and broad-footed amphibians
                        then ground sloths from the south
                        and floods of emigrations from
                            all directions

                bipedal nomads and settlers
                conquerors and missionaries
                men of peace and predators
                refugees and impoverished families
                developers and loud-mouthed parrots
                clamorous and proselytizing
                each thinking they knew the way

and this has been my home
this roof has protected me from the rains
for more years than I have been away

                the first third of my life spent here
            then an equal time spent at camps between
now thirteen more years it will be

before the next full moon begins to wane
following   the footsteps
                                of a scar-nosed hunter

            ∞   ∞   ∞   ∞   ∞

everything in the universe
is racing away from us
away from everything else

this is a given
planets orbit
moons cling like lovers

never turning our faces
we look inward
watch outward

in all directions
seeking clues
our eyesight

following light
redshifted
fireballs racing away

deep lavender good-byes
from ex-lovers
long ago

yet still present
a persistent
background hum

relic radiation
left over from
the initial kiss

the epoch of recombination
like some Platonic reminiscence
or an odd reminiscent old flame

it rings the ears in the quiet hours
to remind of the heat always fading
and disorder being the only end

                    this time

            is all we have

I think

we stare at the light   sent from the suns

billions of dawns

but still

not knowing
anything

it is

all over
for us

we choose explanations most simple
those with the least assumptions

how we come to live apart
should be clear

like the singularity
of one explosion

it was the constant breaking of the heart that has brought me to here
and yet another story has died in my hands

∞   ∞   ∞   ∞

Late at night, passing the front threshold of this house,
a faint chirping   as if a distant echo from above,
an ancient tongue

                forgotten.

I grab a sturdy chair
      shaped out of cherry wood
      by the hands of my grandfather when he was my age,
and drag it outside.

Wedged behind the broken front porch lamp
high on the wall, I see a nest of dried weeds
and twigs that I had failed to remove
      for several seasons,

now reoccupied by squatters.
Earlier in the day I had witnessed the flashing breast of a robin
as it swooped up under the eaves to freshen the nest,
a weed of dead foxtail trailing.

I go back inside and fetch a hand mirror
and flashlight, stand again on the chair,
clinch the penlight between my teeth
and hold the round glass high.

Looking up into the mirror,
I direct the beam with my mouth
as if sunlight to moon,
and bounce the light to flood the nest. *Ah!*

A bald, wrinkled head the size of my knuckle
bobbing between two blue speckled eggs,

chips of broken shell the turquoise of dragonfly,
blue cataract fish-like eyes looking to the false sunrise.

It's a brutal world, little one:
full of terror and full of wonder.
Tingling at the skin and sad to the bone.
But the marrow.

The bigger the brain, the larger the fear, it seems.
Later that night I dream that I am hanging a bird house –
an exact replica of the home behind –
from a nylon line tied to a forking branch of Lacebark Elm,

and suddenly I am tethered, spinning madly
from a beam radiating from the top chakra fontanel,
illuminated only by the moonlight, the prattle
of baby bird cheeps and visions of empty nests

mocking the darkness orbiting my bed.
We spin on such faith, regardless
of name or place or form, balancing sunlight
across the invisible breath,

as if unaware the dark will mute this joyous phase.
One last twisted shine off the filament,
numen spirit of this place, and I feel an inward pull,
as a man who stares out at the ocean might sense

his blood swelling within,
as if the grouping of atoms he is could recall
                         the time of single cell existence,
                         the first pinching off of a gulp
                             of ocean water

                         to enable the oxygenation
                         deeper within, salt sea turning to
                             blood,

                        allowing more complex an organism
                        to develop, evolving more

        over each successive generation,

until we come to this.

The next morning the nest is empty,
robbed by the crows. It is done.
I sweep seasons of dried cocoons
free from eaves, pluck the aerie

from behind the lamp at last,
triangles of broken shell snowing
onto the top of my head, then hose it all clean away
as if it never happened.

                    ∞   ∞   ∞

                    chipped flint arrowhead found in the desert
                    black fur stuck
                    like iron filings on a magnet

it is raining
                            wakook

a dream
                            huuhuvaroy

my image in the water
                            ne'eeshen paanga

the glass holds a bloom

broken tooth unseen below
white feather
grey flint

taste of blood at back of throat

fish's "s" shaped heart
esses
interlinking

cat's fur rosettes

gentle is the instinct
working on the entity
the "s" in sync

rose underbelly of shells

abalone hook
circle arrangement of artifacts
convergence of stories

tokuupng'aro

creaking pink house
stressed then infested
the frame fusing as it ages

peshaax 'ashuun

collapses
back
to earth

peshaax 'akiin

anger in the wind
fighting
lightning

flaring
blue flash
night sky

rancor in the end
nothing
but an aching

limb cracking
tearing
from the trunk alone

the tree
outside
moans

the wind
will not
relent or relate

my arms are heavy
my eyes
tired

and the fires
in the night
insist on blue

∞   ∞

I ask again
for the answer is in
the birthsong of all things
forgotten in waking

yes I want to live again
in the violet
of earthsong sleeping
ease in and out

of breath
and love
uncoiling
to give again

∞

the first drop stains the walk
blackening a circle smelling of earth

a sting on my forehead
the next hits the dirt

I was unaware of the descent above me
as I sat in the fading light of this garden

recalling the day until
one cold slap and then another

a pelting from the sky
clearing circles of focus

explosions on the dirty pane behind me
as if to erase the way for a better view

or to spark some fire

or perhaps to put one out

the butterfly lifts off the post
and disappears over the white fence

my mouth
forms a circle

my throat and tongue
shaping single syllables

in the silence
between drops

mimicking the distinct
sound of each fall

stuh...

puct...
            staw.....

wetting all now
the stones
the soil
my face
until the drops
run down my cheeks
and off of my chin

and he who is mostly water
rises to watch the clouds change form

aware at last
a story was being told
in the skies above
while he sat idle
sung by the rain in
evaporation and precipitation
contraction and release

learning only through its breaking
that the heart is merely an organ of flux

it is not enough to say
all things heal with time
some things can be broken forever
be torn apart so completely
they must become something else
heartwood to ash
memory to stone

tree bark to mold
bone to dust

what once was
can never be again
the only constant
being change
and I feel completion in such things
the flash and rattle of each new beginning
sequoia sprout piercing the dark forest floor

this garden's blades of grass each spring
and the first crack of the bat

(which is but a tree transformed after all)

                              wood whittled to red arrow

                  the whistling from behind

chirping overhead

                              hum from below

                  sinking in of the past

all of it
all of it bringing revelation out of pain

I shall be leaving this place soon

enough

for now

I shall stand with this mystery

I shall keep encouraged

I shall not be apart

NOTES

The author is donating all of his earnings from this book to the Anaheim Heritage Center and MUZEO, the Bowers Museum in Santa Ana, Community of Writers at Squaw Valley, LCAD's Creative Writing Program, Advocates for Indigenous California Language Survival, and other non-partisan nonprofit organizations dedicated to education and egalitarianism, to storytelling, and to keeping alive the cultures and histories that are at the heart of this work.

In that same spirit, what follows is some supplementary material to provide historical context for that which is alluded to in this poem. Included is a guide to those Tongva words and meanings, so that they might be spoken aloud as the poem is read, and remain alive in our consciousness and culture. Of course, the poem alludes to more than just one specific tribe – rather, to all who have dwelt in this place, regardless of when or how we got here, from those first to arrive to the current population. Mitochondrial DNA suggests that the first occupants of North America migrated here more than 12,000 years ago from more than one single homeland, be it Siberia, Western Asia, Europe, or elsewhere – but going back even farther, we now know that the DNA of every human alive today converges on one common "Mitochondrial Eve" mother who lived in Africa, regardless of which creation and migration stories are accurate. This is also alluded to in the poem. The stories of ancestors from the far distant past – about which not much survives but who are a part of our shared continuum, nevertheless – is told in the right column of the poem. The middle column contains the stories of a more recent past, and the left column time-frame is the present day. The people who came to Southern California some 3,500 years ago, who inhabited this place when European colonizers arrived, have been referred to by various names (Tongva, Gabrielino, etc.) and many of these were imposed by outsiders, so there is much debate over what their "proper" name might be (the author's wife is a member of this tribe). Rather than appear to side with any one division, the author hopes instead to focus on that which unites us, the importance of understanding all historical claims and specific cultural heritages, while at the same time recognizing that if we expand the frame, we are all one. Indeed, the poem reaches back beyond bloodline distinctions to the formation of the planet and solar system, the Milky Way before that, even back to the Big Bang. All of our atoms – indeed, all life on Earth – came from residue spewed from stars, and we share 100% of that common bond down to our smallest essence: sisters and brothers all, sharing one home.

Up until the early 1800s there were no records of a written Tongva language. What exists of the vocabulary is based on phonetic representations written down by various speakers of languages other than Tongva. Spellings for the same word differed considerably between those early accounts, which further complicated the task of ascertaining what the words once sounded like. While there are recordings of Tongva music and singing, there are no audio recordings of speech, and the last fluent native speaker died long ago. However, Pamela Munro – the foremost authority in the language and a Distinguished Professor of Linguistics at UCLA – has meticulously compared all records extant and worked with members of the Gabrielino-Tongva Language Committee and other language experts. She has concluded that the diverse spellings in fact represented the same pronunciations, and that we now know with near certainty what these are. It was J. P. Harrington, a trained phonetician and linguist, who provided the most thorough records of the Tongva language, and so his records were used as the standard when examining all versions. By diligently comparing how each different source spelled words for which scholars are fairly certain of the pronunciation, and then standardizing Harrington's spellings for consistency (Harrington himself sometimes used more than one symbol to represent the same sound), Munro has created reliable and consistent spellings for the Tongva language. As they are the most accurate, these are the spellings used herein. Those interested in learning more about indigenous languages are encouraged to explore Munro's books available at Lulu.com (http://www.lulu.com/spotlight/munro1078), her forthcoming *Gabrielino/Tongva/Fernandeño Dictionary*, and the Tongva Language Facebook page, which includes audio recordings of Tongva words and phrases.

While fact checking this manuscript for publication, the author was surprised by the amount of misinformation out there, including vocabulary and histories gathered from seemingly reputable sources but which turned out to be either inaccurate or highly questionable. Rather than risk adding to the "muddy dark" with "unworthy myths" (72) and possibly perpetuating misinformation, the author elected to not include almost all of what could not be verified with certainty. In the few remaining places where there may be dispute, qualifiers such as "some believe" or "some claim" were added to distinguish. Here again, Pam Munro proved invaluable with her sound scholarship and guidance.

What follows is a list of the Tongva words used in this poem, presented in the order they appear, along with their meanings. An apostrophe (') indicates a glottal stop, as in "uh-oh" (or as the "t" is pronounced at the back of the throat when "button" is said fast). Additional information on Tongva pronunciation, as well a study guide for the entire poem, can be found at untended-garden.com and granthier.com

Tongva Word	**Translation**

PAGES 15-17:

Tongva Word	Translation
kakaar	quail
makaaho	mourning dove
piinor	hummingbird: "bringer" (considered a messenger)
che'ee'ax	sing
woshii	dog
tukuut	wildcat
toroovem	dolphins
'akuutesh	butterfly
yakeenax	dance (verb)
yovaareka'	One of two shamans of the Tongva. *Ahuuhvarot* made medicines and read people's dreams. *Yovaareka'* was the storytelling shaman, preserving the tribal past (from *yovaar* meaning "church" or, presumably, "sacred place"). He also created new songs, dances, and poems to document new histories for future remembrance.
nenaak	my father
nyook	my mother
nemaaman	my hands
ne'een	my bone
neshuun	my heart
nexaayn	my blood
'wee	all
'ooxor	ground, earth
mamaahar	grass
yaawket	night
mwaar	moon
shushuu'ram	stars

yataamkok	sleep (verb)
kivaa'	old house
yovaareka'	the storytelling shaman (see above)
'ekwaa	here
yuupet	overcast
'akwaaken	rain
paar	water
wenoot	stream
paxaayt	river
'ahaavkomen paar	seashore, surf: "the edge of the water"
nemaaman	my hands (see above)
yovaareka'	the storytelling shaman (see above)

PAGE 45:

paxuuche'	A bird-bone whistle – as played by the "bird-bone whistler." The UCLA Fowler Museum of Cultural History has a "Gabrielino bird bone whistle" in their archives (L. 10.7 cm x W. 0.6 cm x Th. 0.6 cm).

PAGE 58:

konaashnga	burial ground or cemetery
koshiiy	ashes
tayiiy honuuka'	ancestor
'wee 'eyoohiinkem	all our relatives

"People of the Earth"

What the Gabrieleno/Tongva Nation claims "Tongva" means. Along with the missionary-given "Gabrielino," Tongva is the most commonly used name for the tribe that moved into Southern California some 3,500 years ago.

"Indigenous People of the (Willow) Brush Houses"

What the Kizh Nation Gabrieleño Band of Mission Indians refer to themselves as (rejecting both "Tongva" and "Gabrielino").

"Place of the Poison Oak"

The translation of the Luiseño word *Iyala*, and perhaps as *Iyakha* is what the Luiseño called the Tongva village where downtown Los Angeles now stands (*Yaanga*).

"Beautiful People" and "Those Covered Ones"

Two translations of the Serrano word *Havakam* (in the *Pipimarra'yam* dialect and *Muhanyam* dialect, respectively). This is what the Serrano called the Tongva peoples.

"Those With the Long Arms"

What the Buena Vista Lake Hometwoli (Hammetwelle) Yokuts speakers called the Tongva peoples (from *miyahhiktchallop* "long arms").

Ywaat

"Snow" or "Snowy Mountain," what some claim the Tongva called Mount Baldy as one of their Four Sacred Mountains. "The place below Snowy Mountain," or *Tooro' Ywaanga*, was the Tongva village that occupied present-day Claremont.

'Akwaanga

What some claim the Tongva called Mt. San Gorgonio as one of their Four Sacred Mountains.

Yamiwu

What some claim the Tongva called Mt. San Jacinto as one of their Four Sacred Mountains (although this does not appear to be a Tongva word, according to Munro).

Har'wovet

What some claim the Tongva called Mt. Saddleback as one of their Four Sacred Mountains (although this does not appear to be a Tongva word, according to Munro).

Paayme Paxaayt   "West River," what some claim the Tongva called the Los Angeles River as one of their Four Sacred Rivers. The *Yaanga* tribe of downtown referred to the Los Angeles River as *'Ochoo' Paxaayt*, or "Cold River."

Chinuuy Paxaayt   "Little River," what some claim the Tongva called the Rio Hondo as one of their Four Sacred Rivers. Really a tributary of the Los Angeles River running from Irwindale to South Gate – a parallel channel of the San Gabriel River flowing through Whittier Narrows.

Totootanga Paxaayt   "In the Rocks River," what some claim the Tongva called the San Gabriel River as one of their Four Sacred Rivers.

Kahoo' Paxaayt   "Long River," what some claim the Tongva called the Santa Ana River as one of their Four Sacred Rivers. The Santa Ana River is, in fact, the longest river in Southern California.

Pakooynga   "At the Entrance" (from *pakook* "enter"), the Tongva village thought to be the source of the name Pacoima.

Tuhuunga   "Place of the Old Woman" (from *tuxuu'* "old woman"), later becoming Tujunga. Some see this as referring to the "mountain home of old woman," or Mother Earth.

'Ashuukshanga   "The Place of the Grandmother" (from *'ashuuk* "his grandmother"). This was the source of the name Azusa, which is what that place is called now.

Yaanga   A Tongva village that occupied present-day downtown Los Angeles.

Povuu'nga   A Tongva village that occupied present-day eastern Long Beach, Los Alamitos, Rossmoor, Seal Beach, Cypress, Stanton, and Garden Grove. Some Tongva believe this is where the Creator God sang and danced the Tongva people into being, near what is now known as Bixby Hill at the northern border of California State University, Long Beach.

Lukuupanga   What some claim was the name of the Tongva village in present-day Huntington Beach.

Xaaxamonga   A Tongva village that contained the upper Arroyo Seco area, present-day Pasadena, Glendale, Burbank, also known as "Rancho de los Verdugos."

Mayoonga	A Tongva village that occupied present-day Corona Del Mar, Balboa, Laguna.
Kawee'nga	A Tongva village in or near present-day San Fernando Valley, later becoming Cahuenga.
Kuukamonga	A Tongva village in or near present-day San Gabriel Valley, later becoming Cucamonga.
Topaa'nga	A Tongva village that occupied present-day Malibu, later becoming Topanga.
Hotuuknga	A Tongva village that occupied present-day La Habra, Yorba Linda, Anaheim, Santa Ana.

PAGES 86-87:

wakook	it is raining
huuhuvaroy	a dream
ne'eeshen paanga	my image in the water
tokuupng'aro	"to the sky" or "to heaven" (sometimes translated as "final abode," "future world," or "place above").
peshaax 'ashuun	"his heart leaves" (sometimes translated as "spirit while in body").
peshaax 'akiin	"his house leaves" (sometimes translated as "spirit after leaving body").

"FOURTEEN-POINTED COG STONE / ABALONE SHELL ANOINTMENT"

It was this exact 14-pointed cog stone (right) that the author saw at Bowers Museum, which inspired him to include it in the poem (on page 15). Usually found on ocean bluffs or other coastal hilly areas, cog stones (or "cogged stones") were found throughout Southern California, including large deposits along the Santa Ana River valley. Similar stones have been found in the coastal areas of Chile and Peru. This 14-pointed stone and the group of cog stones pictured below date back approximately 8,000 years, long before the Tongva peoples arrived in Southern California. They are attributed to the ancient and non-nomadic people of the Milling Stone Horizon culture.

No one knows exactly what these stones were used for. They vary in shape, size, and number of teeth. Some seem more polished, others rough. Some have holes at the center, others do not. There are no discernable patterns of wear. They may have had religious or astronomical applications, demonstrating rhythms of nature perhaps, or were used in rituals or magic. Some think they are representations of marine life. They may also have been used in sand paintings, or in other art making, or as jewelry or decoration. Or, they might have been used in games. Others think they might have been used as tools, perhaps to weigh down fishing nets; they seem too soft to be used for striking or grinding. Some believe the cogs indicate they were an aid in manufacturing rope, but no traces of accompanying fiber have been found. The stones are rarely found with other objects nearby. They remain a mystery.

ABOVE:
Cog Stone, suggested date 6000-3500 B.C.
Milling Stone Horizon Peoples; Southern California;
Object Number 477; Scoria; 3 5/8 x 1 1/2 in.
Courtesy of the Bowers Museum, Santa Ana, CA

LEFT:
Top row Cog Stones, suggested date 6000-3500 B.C.
Milling Stone Horizon Peoples; Southern California;
Object Numbers (viewer's left to right): 11677, 1825, 11644, 11641, 11666
Bottom row (viewer's left to right): 11652, N40, 80001, N367, 80002
Various stones including basalt; average dimension: 3 3/4 x 1 1/2 in.
Courtesy of the Bowers Museum, Santa Ana, CA

DOWNTOWN LOS ANGELES AND THE COUNCIL TREE "*EL ALISO*" IN 1850

Looking northeast, the layout of the new city can clearly be seen with the Los Angeles Plaza located in the lower left-center. The large white structure to the left of the Plaza is the Old Plaza Church. The two streets running from bottom of photo to the Plaza are Main Street on the left and Los Angeles Street on the right. Alameda Street runs from the lower right corner diagonally toward the lower center of photo.

The L.A. River can be seen running from the lower-right diagonally to the center of the photo, turns left and disappears behind the mountain. At that point the Arroyo Seco can be seen at its confluence with the LA River. The tall majestic San Gabriel Mountains stand in the far background. Vineyards blanket the area between the City and the L.A. River (lower right quadrant).

The sycamore tree *El Aliso* can be seen as the oblong black mass near the river in the lower right of the image on the opposite page (a little less than 1" up from the bottom and .75" from the right border). For at least 400 years this giant tree was a historic landmark of the Tongva people who once lived in the village of *Yaanga* at that location, adjacent to the L.A. River.

On August 15, 1895, when the tree was being chopped down, the *Los Angeles Herald* reported that *El Aliso* stood at least 125 feet in height, and measured over seven feet in diameter, twenty-two feet in circumference, with "mammoth roots" that extended more than 60-80 feet in all directions. This tree was the benchmark starting point from which the Tongva calculated distances and the boundary lines of property, and "was to be seen from all the peaks and plains in the surrounding country."

She is mentioned on page 64 of the poem, and her rise and fall is described on pages 73-77.

RIGHT:
The first plaza area in Los Angeles, as it appeared in 1850
Picture file card identifies the image as a diorama of the Pueblo Los Angeles as it appeared in 1850 as designed by J. Marshall Miller. Picture file card also reads "Prepared for the Los Angeles Times Anniversary 1931?".

Digitally reproduced by the USC Digital Library
From the California Historical Society Collection at the University of Southern California ; "USC Digital Library." Used with permission.

A high resolution (zoomable) version of this image can be found at
http://digitallibrary.usc.edu/cdm/singleitem/collection/p15799coll65/id/25374/rec/1

"THIS FROSTLESS ZONE SO PRONE TO OVERFLOWING"

FLOOD REFERENCES ON PAGES 58-59, 74 AND ELSEWHERE

The Department of Public Works, Los Angeles, has an excellent summary of the history of this region and its water, available online at http://dpw.lacounty.gov/wmd/watershed/LA/History.cfm. What follows is a brief overview, paraphrasing sections of that source and adding other details related to specific histories called up in the poem:

Going back tens of million of years, what is now Los Angeles and Orange County was shallow ocean bottom (alluded to on page 14 and elsewhere). As the mountain ranges formed and the land rose to the topography familiar to us today, the Los Angeles basin received massive amounts of watershed draining from the top of what we now call the San Fernando Valley and the San Gabriel Mountains, Santa Monica Mountains, and Santa Susana Mountains – as well as the natural artisan flow of fresh groundwater from under the rivers – and as such became a rich landscape of dense flora and fauna. Those who migrated here thousands of years ago found the many riversides ideal settlements. In 1542, Juan Cabrillo of Portugal observed haze above San Pedro Bay and dubbed the region "Bay of Smokes." In 1602, Sebastian Vizcaino of Spain intermingled with the coastal inhabitants, and 160 years later Gaspar de Portola described a village of several hundred on the site of present day Los Angeles City Hall – although this village, *Yaanga*, continually moved camp according to the changing landscape, their wickiup houses easily re-assembled yet always near the river. Portola established a Spanish riverside settlement as well, naming the river "*Rio de Nuestra Senora la Reina de los Angeles de Porciuncula*" (River of Our Lady Queen of the Angels of Porciuncula).

The history of Southern California is one of constant change and repeated flooding. Time and again, uncontrolled runoff saturated the lands and swelled creeks and rivers, enabling newer, less-resistant water routes downhill to the sea. The San Gabriel River once emptied into the ocean via the current path of the Los Angeles River, and the Los Angeles River changed course several times, from draining westward into the Santa Monica Bay (via Ballona Creek), to run more southward. The *Yaanga* settlement and the original *Pueblo de Los Angeles* were destroyed by an 1815 flood. In 1825 a massive flood formed vast swamps leading to the ocean (south of downtown), and eventually the river diverted toward those swamps and found a new outlet to the Pacific, near the present-day Port of Long Beach. Channelization of the river began in 1938, and by 1960 the Los Angeles River became 51 miles of engineered waterway with water treatment plants, straightening to a mostly man-made route, existing now as a concrete run-off channel, no longer directly feeding the soil.

The wild and seasonally unpredictable rivers of Southern California, controlled and reshaped in the name of utilitarianism, are still being transformed by man. Restoration and redevelopment projects are evolving, and debates continue over a river's function and who should design and control any changes, who should have

access, and who should benefit the most. Even though rivers don't naturally run
year round, some argue for a controlled year-round flow to allow for new housing
with public parks, new enterprise, and further industrialization. Others seek
restoration that values sustainability and ecology above other interests, perhaps even
removing concrete banks completely, allowing rerouting and re-naturalization closer
to the river's natural state, which would certainly benefit wildlife – and perhaps all
flora and fauna.

SANTA ANA RIVER FLOOD, 1916:

The Santa Ana River supplied agricultural Orange County with most of its irrigation
water, but often overflowed its banks. This photograph was taken near the corner of
Magnolia and Lincoln (near where the Carbon Creek Channel Tributary cuts across
what is now Dad Miller Golf Course), some 400 feet east and 2600 feet north of the
author's home and the setting of this story. Hidden beneath these muddy waters are
the yet-to-be-developed lots and gardens of mid-century housing tracts to come.

Flood of 1916, Anaheim.
Courtesy of the Anaheim Public Library;
Anaheim Heritage Center (plate 15027).

A NOTE ON THE DESIGN

This book uses the font Minion Pro, a typeface inspired by calligraphy and late Renaissance type, with large apertures for readability, humanist axis tilt, flowing adnate serifs, elegant long descenders, and fine details that echo natural pen strokes.

All cover photography and book design by Grant Hier.

Cover:

> The bark of the Chinese Elm tree (Lace Elm) in the front yard of the author's home, as mentioned on pages 4, 31, 37-38, and 85.

Back Cover:

> Left Image – Concrete fossil of a Balm of Gilead Cottonwood leaf (the tree itself no longer remaining) in the back yard of the author's home. The parent tree and its offshoots are mentioned on pages 5, 31, and 47.

> Center Image – Plat of housing development tract number 2874, Orange County, California (subdivision filed with the City of Anaheim on March 28, 1956). The author's home can be seen at the top (subdivision 57). Note the well site located in the back yard, mentioned on page 80.

> Right Image – Untended garden leaves, figs and soil in the back yard of the author's home.

ACKNOWLEDGMENTS

Thanks to Galway Kinnell and Gary Snyder for their counsel on working in the long poem genre, and Gary again for the dialogue on the theme of Reinhabitation and encouraging my pursuit of applying it to suburbia. Galway, I wish you could have seen how this poem took root after we talked.

Thanks to Pattiann Rogers and the Community of Writers at Squaw Valley for providing insight on the most difficult sections.

Thanks to Gerald Locklin and Charles Harper Webb for their direct feedback on the first draft of this poem some twenty years ago, and for their great inspiration and mentoring at a crucial time in my poetic career.

Thanks to Pamela Munro for her generous help in ensuring the accuracy of the Tongva language contained herein.

Very special thanks to Leslie Kreiner Wilson, Executive Director and Editor-in-Chief at Americana, for the freedom she afforded me. Also, for her conscientious work ensuring that such storytelling and scholarship survives.

Beyond this poem, thanks to the members of our long-standing poetry workshop (which originated at Squaw Valley), especially my fellow co-founders Rosemarie Johnstone and Lorene Delany-Ullman.

Lifelong thanks to Peggy Hesketh, and all of the others who have made me a better writer. You know who you are.

Lastly, endless gratitude and love to my father Stanley, mother Gloria, sister Suzan, and wife Laura – for everything.

GRANT HIER

In addition to winning the 2014 PRIZE AMERICANA for this book, Grant Hier is also recipient of the 2014 NANCY DEW TAYLOR PRIZE for Literary Excellence in Poetry, and the 2013 KICK PRIZE. His poems have been widely published internationally, including in *Emrys Journal, Dallas Review, Poetry Digest, Poets Against the War, Zócalo Public Square, WTC Remembrances, Review Americana, Pearl, Poetry/LA, Chiron Review, Blue Fifth Review Quarterly, Orange County Review, Orange Coast Review, RipRap, Re)verb, Slipstream, City Dialogues, Tandava, Faith, Stymie, Word Riot,* and others. His poetry will be anthologized in the Knopf/Everyman volume *Human and Inhuman Poems,* and he will have three flash fiction pieces included in the Red Hen Press *Anthology of Los Angeles Short Fiction.* His fiction, reviews, and essays have been widely published as well, including in *Jeffers Studies, The Review of Contemporary Fiction, Teaching Composition with Literature, Explorations in English Studies,* and the award-winning book, *John Fante: A Critical Gathering.* He has served as editor of several literary journals and magazines. In addition to writing, he is a musical artist, visual artist, graphic designer, and former Art Director. He recorded his original musical compositions for A&M Records in Los Angeles, and his installation art has been featured in several gallery showings. Grant earned his MA in Literature and MFA in Creative Writing Poetry at CSULB, and he currently teaches creative writing, literature, and various other courses at Laguna College of Art + Design in Laguna Beach where he is Professor of English and Chair of Liberal Arts and Art History. He is currently developing an MFA Program in Creative Writing at LCAD. He lives in Anaheim with his wife Laura, in the very home that is the *axis mundi* of this poem.